# A Day With A
# MILLER

# A Day With A
# Miller

by Régine Pernoud

Illustrations by Giorgio Bacchin
Translated by Dominique Clift

**RP**

Runestone Press/Minneapolis
A Division of the Lerner Publishing Group

All words that appear in **bold** are explained in the
glossary that starts on page 43.

This edition first published in the United States in 1997 by Runestone Press.

Copyright © 1996 Editoriale Jaca Book SpA, Milano. All rights reserved. Originally
produced in 1996 by Editoriale Jaca Book, Milan, Italy.

Runestone Press, c/o The Lerner Publishing Group
241 First Avenue North, Minneapolis, MN 55401 U.S.A.

Photo on p. 15 is used courtesy of Zodiaque.

Library of Congress Cataloging-in-Publication Data

Pernoud, Régine.
[Mugnaio medievale. English]
A miller / by Régine Pernoud ; illustrated by Giorgio Bacchin.
p.   cm.   —(A day with—)
Includes index, bibliographical references.
Summary: Describes, both factually and fictionally, a day in
the life of a miller in medieval Europe.
ISBN 0–8225–1914–3 (lib. bdg. : acid-free paper)
1. Grain—Milling—Europe—History—Juvenile literature.
2. Millers—Europe—Juvenile literature. 3. Middle Ages—Europe—
Juvenile literature. [1. Millers.  2. Middle Ages.]  I. Bacchin,
Giorgio, ill.   II. Title.   III. Series.
TS2135.E85P4713   1997
664'.72'0094—dc20      96–28160
CIP
Manufactured in the United States of America
1 2 3 4 5 6 - JR - 02 01 00 99 98 97

# CONTENTS

# INTRODUCTION

*Middle Ages* and *medieval* are terms that refer to a period in European history. This period, which lasted from roughly A.D. 500 to A.D. 1500, is sandwiched between the Roman Empire and the **Renaissance,** or rebirth of interest in classical Greece and Rome. The ideas that took root during the Renaissance mark the beginning of the modern era of Europe's history.

During the Middle Ages, the lives of the people of Europe were focused around two important factors—the power of the **Roman Catholic Church** and the power of the **landowners.** These two factors shaped European society.

The church, in addition to taking care of religious matters, offered opportunities for education, fostered the arts (such as music and sculpture), and supported massive building projects. People at every level of medieval life held strongly to Catholic beliefs, and the decorations on churches were symbols of this faith and devotion.

The landowners—usually noble lords who lived in castles—held power under a governing system known as **feudalism.** Although a lord might owe loyalty to a king, within his own territory, the lord managed agriculture, trade, and industry. He collected taxes, demanded military service, and made judicial decisions.

Most ordinary people, known as **peasants,** lived and worked on the lord's land and had few rights. They tilled his soil, cut his wood, repaired his buildings—in short they did whatever the lord asked of them. In return, the lord provided peace and security. Some commoners—mainly merchants and **artisans**—were residents of towns. By about the eleventh century—the beginning of the **High Middle Ages**—Europe had many towns and several large cities. The first towns had been set up near castles, but as local trade grew, towns also developed along rivers and other commercial routes. Peasants began to leave rural areas to find jobs in towns. Craftworkers, merchants, food vendors, and innkeepers made up the towns' populations. Some peasants farmed their own land outside the towns and provided the townspeople with food.

This story of a medieval miller takes place during the High Middle Ages in Beaugency, a town in north central France. Millers were among the first professionals to exist independently from the feudal estates, and mills were important parts of medieval communities. Although mills have changed since the Middle Ages, updated versions of the mill in this story are still used in modern times.

*Series Editors*

# PART ONE

# THE WORLD OF A MEDIEVAL MILLER

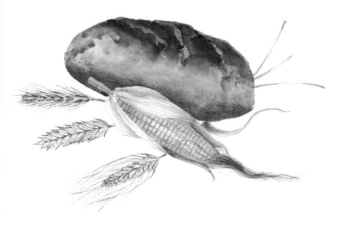

Since the earliest days of civilization, bread has been a basic source of nourishment. Thousands of years ago, grinding wheat to make flour was the task of slaves or women. Grinding was generally done with a round millstone, rotated by hand around a central point.

*People began storing grain, already known in its wild form, as early as 10,000 B.C. and began growing crops, such as wheat and corn, around 8000 B.C. The illustration (above) shows an ear of **wild cereal**, along with varieties of **cultivated cereals**, and a loaf of baked bread.*

(Above) *Millstones were among the earliest grinding tools. Workers crushed the grain between two rocks by pulling a long, narrow stone across a flat stone. Although time-consuming, this method of grinding was common throughout the world and is still in use among traditional peoples in Africa, Asia, and the Americas.*

(Right) *A more complex mill, called a **quern**, was later developed. Instead of a simple back and forth movement, a quern had a circular motion that was produced by turning the top stone with a peg or handle. Using a handle to rotate the stone required less effort and was more effective than the earlier millstone.*

Conditions in medieval Europe—such as geography, climate, local needs, and foreign influence—led to the adoption of more advanced technologies in milling. Many different types of mills existed. (Right) A waterfall was one way to power a wheel connected to a millstone. (Below) A more common method, though, was to build the wheel and mill along a fast-flowing stream. The flow of the river turned the waterwheel (A) to which another wheel (B) was attached by an axle. This second wheel had wooden teeth sticking out one side that fit into a wooden gear (C). As the waterwheel turned, the teeth meshed with the gear, which was connected to the **grindstone** (D). The grain was poured through a hole in the roof into the **hopper** (E). The hopper funneled the grain to a hole in the grindstone. The movement of the grindstone above a fixed stone (F) spread out the grain and ground it into flour.

(Above) *Each millstone had a system of grooves that, when the grindstone turned, cut and ground the grain.* (Below) *Millstones required regular maintenance. In humid weather, ground and pulverized grain got sticky and left residue inside the grooves. The miller had to clean the millstones carefully, otherwise the residue would clog the grooves, making it difficult to grind again.*

# TECHNOLOGICAL INNOVATIONS AND SOCIAL CHANGE

People in the Middle Ages utilized natural energy resources, particularly water power. Use of **hydraulic energy** drastically affected the technological advances and economic progress that took place in the medieval period.

Water power wasn't extensively used until the Middle Ages. Medieval engineers took full advantage of Europe's tight network of waterways. From the tenth century onward, thousands of water mills churned along the banks of European rivers and waterfalls.

*This illustration* (above) *depicts a water mill, from a twelfth-century manuscript by Herrard of Landsberg, Germany. A medieval mill was a considerable investment. The costly building had complex machinery* (left) *that was expensive to install and repair. A miller also needed a supply of spare parts for maintenance in this small business enterprise. The mill generally was located on a feudal estate and was rented to the miller for a yearly payment of flour.*

Advances in technology also brought social change, especially to the feudal system of rights and privileges. Under the feudal system, **tenants** were required to work for the lord and to give him the fruits of their harvest. Until the invention of water-powered mills, peasants used querns or millstones to prepare grain manually. When mill technology became more complex, lords looked beyond the labor of their estates and gave the job to a miller. Because millers had invaluable and specialized skills, feudal lords granted them independence from the estate. Millers eventually operated communal mills and extended their services to townspeople, **abbeys,** and other nobles. Millers made yearly payments of flour to the castles of their overlords as a form of rent for using the mill.

In a sense, then, millers were early entrepreneurs—people who learned how to market their services and to improve the productivity of their machinery. The technology of the mill was eventually applied to producing other goods such as tanning animal pelts, brewing beer, forging iron, and manufacturing textiles.

Although advances in mill technology ended certain types of manual labor, the improvements also created opportunities for artisans and technicians. A class of independent workers who were skilled in maintaining machinery grew alongside the development of new technologies.

*Medieval peasants* (above) *led a hard life. Feudal lords demanded heavy payment in goods from their tenants who farmed the land. After paying the lord, these peasant families often hadn't enough food to feed themselves. Independent farmers lived on plots that frequently were too small to support them. After a bad season or two, overwhelmed by poverty and debt, these farmers had no choice but to accept **servitude** on a feudal estate. In this way, feudal lords ensured themselves an ongoing supply of labor and goods.*

*The miller was a new figure in medieval society. When millers set up their own businesses, they were no longer dependent on a feudal castle or an abbey. They might even have had hired help. A successful miller could have had a garden, a cowshed, and a poultry coop that supplied his family with food. Bread, the product of his work, cost him very little.*

Towers sprang up near castles to support the new class of artisans, merchants, and independent workers (right) who were leaving servitude. Medieval millers provided goods and services to many customers from the nearby town. Families, bakers, and members of religious and **secular** orders all went to a mill to have their cereal ground into flour for bread, cakes, or **semolina.** Millers also hired artisans to build dams, dykes, embankments, or walls to control the flow of water. To the miller's benefit, these artisans helped repair and modernize the mills, making them even more efficient business enterprises. Mills not only provided a way of life for the millers but were also important in stimulating local economic activity.

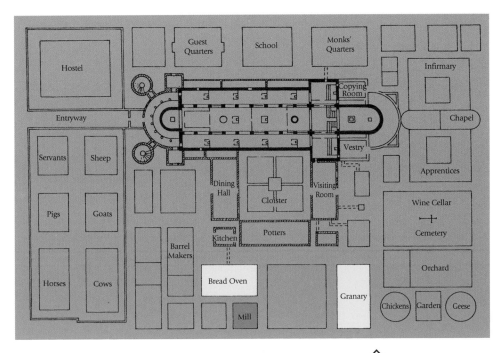

Castles were not the only establishments to have mills. Large abbeys did, too. The plan (left) of the Abbey of St. Gall—a **Benedictine** abbey in the Swiss Alps—shows the area reserved for the mill. Abbeys could be completely self-sufficient. Other religious communities, however, such as the one in the story that follows, had to rely on outside suppliers. These communities depended on independent millers and also on other artisans that operated in the growing secular economy.

The tight network of European waterways (above) fostered the development of hydraulic energy.
The Middle Ages saw a rapid expansion of water mill activity.

Improved water technology boosted construction of mills along waterways. The miller soon became a familiar and important figure in medieval society. Landry, the fictional twelfth-century miller in the story that follows, lived and worked in Beaugency, France, on the banks of the Loire River.

(Above) *This twelfth-century* **capital,** *or sculpted head of a column, comes from the Basilica of Vézelay, in France. The carving depicts a miller grinding grain. The miller's occupation had a great deal of prestige in the Middle Ages.*

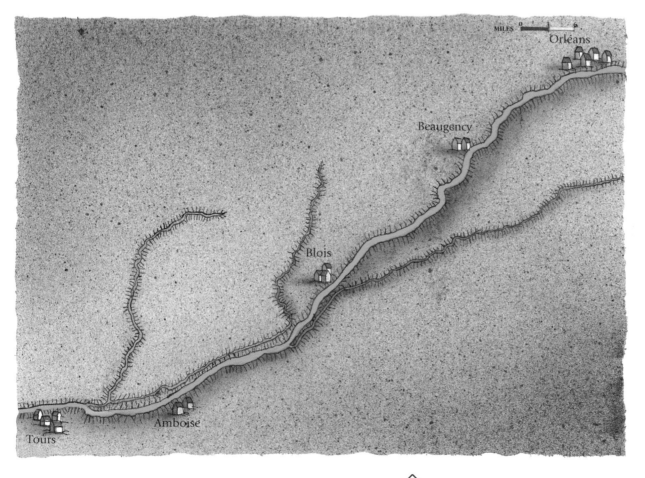

(Left) *This illustration shows the course of the Loire River. Its abundant waters, with strong potential for channelling, were an important source of hydroelectric power to the emerging industries of France.*

Although fictionalized, the story of Landry, a twelfth-century miller, and his family is drawn from historical accounts. Landry and his family live in Beaugency, a town along the Loire River just south of the city of Orléans. Landry's mill is part of the feudal estate of the lord of Beaugency. The lord gives Landry the freedom to use the mill in exchange for a percentage of the flour the miller grinds each year.

Because he is the only miller in town, Landry gets business from all the local townspeople, as well as from nearby St. George's Abbey. Landry's eldest son, Gregory, helps run the mill. Gregory will probably take charge of the mill when he is old enough. Running a mill is hard work. The miller must make sure the mill's parts are clean and in good repair. He must also keep up with his customers' demands for flour.

Let's join Landry and his family in a typical day in the life of a medieval miller. . .

# PART TWO

# A Day with Landry, a Twelfth-Century Miller

**T**he rooster had just started crowing. Landry opened his eyes. In June the nights were short, and he already sensed the faint light of dawn. Far away the bells of Notre-Dame Abbey were ringing. It was time to get up.

Landry moved carefully. The children were still asleep. So was his wife, Françoise. He stepped quietly out of the bedroom and crept down the stairs. He went to the well at the back of the house to draw some water with a pail tied to the end of a rope. He washed vigorously but made a face at the coldness of the water. Being a miller required cleanliness. Nothing sticks to the skin like flour or, even worse, the **bran** that separates from the coarse flour during sifting. But life was not so hard at this time of year. All around him, the water trickled off into the meadow where the hens and chickens would soon be pecking away.

**A**fter drying himself, he went back into the house where Françoise was already reviving the embers of last night's fire. Landry sat down at the table. He began each morning with a bowl of leftover soup, a piece of crunchy bread, and a glass of wine. He was ready to start the mill for another day's work.

By that time, almost the entire household was awake. Gregory, the firstborn, appeared. His father sent him outside to wash—a good habit more easily acquired in summertime. Gregory worked at the mill as his father's assistant. The family also included ten-year-old twin boys, Isaac and Damian. This summer they attended a class held by the priest of nearby St. Étienne Church, where they were learning to sing, read, and write.

Nanon, a distant relative of Françoise, was also a part of the household. After being widowed and left penniless, she was taken in by Françoise. Every morning Nanon went out to milk the cows. When she returned, everyone sat down with large mugs of warm milk and slices of bread and honey. Only Clémence, Landry's six-year old daughter, was still asleep. Everyone tiptoed so as not to wake her.

Waving good-bye to the twins, Landry made his way to the mill. A narrow channel next to the mill house brought enough water to turn the grinding wheel. The lord of Beaugency had built the mill when Landry's grandfather was alive. The mill had a tall square tower, which was the pride of the whole countryside. For generations, the mill had been communal property on the feudal estate. But years ago, the heir to the estate signed it over to Landry in return for bags of flour to be delivered every autumn on St. Michael's Day. Many more mills had since appeared along the Loire, but Landry's business was well situated on the river, and he had many loyal customers.

The only problem with the milling business occurred when water levels were low during dry spells in summer. Although the problem had happened a few times, Landry used a dry spell as an opportunity to clean the river channel and to lay stones to support its banks. This year there was nothing to worry about. The Loire was running high after a rainy spring.

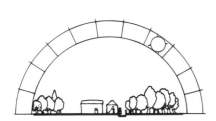

When at last Clémence came down for her bowl of warm milk, the grinding wheel was already rumbling as it would for the rest of the day. There were plenty of other noises, too. Goats bleated, hens clucked, and the family dog barked. Ducks quacked on their way to the water, and turtledoves cooed endlessly. Along with Nanon, Clémence went out to collect some eggs, which she carried back in her apron. She could spot the eggs from a distance. The hens seemed to have fun laying eggs in unexpected places as if they were playing treasure hunt.

Upon seeing Gregory in a window of the mill, Clémence smiled and waved. He was already at work, handling a hopper. She wanted to visit him but was not allowed to get close to the mill's **headrace,** where the current was strong and the grass was wet and slippery. No one wanted Clémence to risk falling into the water. Then she saw a woman at the foot of the stairs—the first customer of the day.

Landry recognized her right away. "Hey, Mrs. Matthieu," he said in greeting. "I hope this isn't **spelt** you're bringing this time?"

"Don't worry," the woman replied. "It's a peck of oats. Every day my mother wants her porridge. She says it's more easily digested than wheat!"

Landry gave a sigh of relief. Eight days ago, Mrs. Matthieu had brought some spelt, and to make things worse this tough wheat had been poorly dried. After the job, he'd had to stop the wheel to clean the stones with a feather from the rooster's wing. The sticky bran had caught in the fine grooves of the wheel. The result was coarse oatmeal instead of flour. Landry had always taken pride in turning out the finest flour, suitable for both bread and buns. He had warned her that spelt needed to be dried well in the oven before milling. But customers didn't understand these things!

"It will be just a few minutes, Mrs. Matthieu. It's the baker's turn."

The baker always had priority over other customers. Of course, he already had a batch of bread in the oven, but he thought he might need extra flour for tomorrow. His **apprentice** was waiting next to the mill with a donkey.

Another customer showed up carrying half a bag of rye. She started explaining to Mrs. Matthieu that bread tastes better when you add a bit of rye to the wheat. The young baker's apprentice shook his head in disapproval: another family baking their bread at home when they could just as well buy it already made.

Meanwhile, Clémence burst in to the kitchen, breathless. "Look what I found," she cried to her mother, opening her apron. "Strawberries! There are tons of them at the edge of the woods," Clémence explained.

"I will bake a pie for tonight. This will be a surprise for Isaac and Damian when they come back. Don't tell them anything, not even Gregory. We'll make the pie together this afternoon," her mother proposed.

It was lunchtime. Landry found joy in his daughter who kissed him before settling down for lunch. Gregory was still at the mill keeping an eye on the oats being ground. He was expected for lunch later. Father and son routinely replaced one another at the mill. Françoise had prepared roast pork with peas. She had spent part of the morning making butter. She'd also prepared curdled goat milk for the cheese rounds that were then stored in the cellar. They'd be ready to eat in a few days.

Because the twins spent the whole day at St. Étienne, they couldn't join the family meal. Instead they brought with them a thick slice of ham between slices of buttered bread. They could supplement their meal with wild fruits, which were plentiful in summer along the Loire.

It was a noisy afternoon at the mill. Two **lay brothers** from St. George's Abbey were driving six donkeys. Each animal carried two sacks on its back. At the top of their voices, the monks were calling on every saint in heaven to keep the donkeys moving. A large number of other customers were waiting for their flour. Mrs. Matthieu was back with a neighbor to fetch her oat flour. Both were mocking another person waiting to be served, a bearded and serious-looking peasant. Their words caused him to turn around abruptly and give them a menacing look. Gregory thought he heard one of the women say, "He would do better to keep an eye on his daughter than on his flour."

Gregory knew the daughter, who enjoyed hearing compliments from the boys. Landry reacted immediately: "You **gossips,** cut it out! It's your fault that the parish priest is down on me. In his sermon, didn't he speak about rumor at the mill? Go home if you can't hold your tongues. It would be better than stirring up bad feelings."

The gossips suppressed their laughter, exchanging knowing glances while the bearded peasant hurried home. Landry turned to the monks unloading sacks from their donkeys.

"All that by tonight? You should have come earlier! Is it wheat?"

"No, it's a mixed crop of wheat and rye, Landry. You know we aren't allowed to have bread, unless we are ill or whenever the abbot has guests. These sacks are all we have left. Thank God the new crop will soon be in."

Landry immediately got to work, which would earn him a half a sack of the grain. It was a hard job removing the bran from the flour in this type of mixture. And here were the monks bringing twelve sacks. "We'll be working until nightfall! Not a moment to lose, Gregory!" Fortunately, the days are long in June.

As was the custom, the miller was paid in kind rather than money. He generally got one-twelfth of what people brought him to grind. Sometimes he only received one-sixteenth, if it happened to be high-quality wheat.

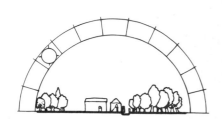

**L**andry was a hard worker, and many people believed he was wealthy. The truth was he always put a lot of energy into whatever he did. And so did his wife, who managed the small farm that produced the family's meals. They also had two cows, a few goats, some chickens, and a pig that thrived on table scraps. By some standards, the miller and his family lived well, but they spared neither time nor effort.

The evening meal brought the whole family together, including Isaac and Damian, who were very excited on their return from St. Étienne.

"Daddy, tomorrow is a holiday. It's **St. Peter's Day!**" they said together.

Landry had forgotten about that. It was a good thing he'd finished grinding the sacks brought in by the monks. "We're putting on a play at the beginning of August, for next St. Peter's Day. We will be playing the life of Job," the twins announced, still very excited. The parish priest of St. Étienne occasionally asked them to act out scenes from the Bible so the stories stayed vivid in their minds. "I will be playing Job," Damian proclaimed.

"And you, Isaac, who are you playing?"

"A friend of Job. He tells him nasty things that will make him angry."

"This is very interesting," said Françoise. "Naturally we will go see you both in the play. But for now, let's have this pot of chicken with cabbage. And there is a surprise for desert," she added, winking at Clémence who responded by clapping her hands.

At first Landry was upset at the prospect of a holiday. But he came around to the idea of some rest after a hard day's work. And the whole family cheered the strawberry pie that Françoise brought to the table.

The family lingered through the evening, not around the fireplace as in winter, but outside on a stone bench set near the front door. The animals were already in their pens. The boys had a great time playing leapfrog on the meadow close to the house. Watching the children play, Landry had an idea.

**T**omorrow is a holiday," he said, "and I'll have time to set up a game of **quintain** for you. You can play being knights. We'll see who is most skillful!"

Whoops of joy greeted Landry. Soon it was nightfall, and everyone went to bed.

# AFTERWORD

The development of the water mill, one of the most important inventions of the Middle Ages, was accompanied by technological and social change. Mills like the one Landry operated stayed much the same until the sixteenth century, when higher demands for flour spurred the search for new ways to achieve large-scale production.

New innovations meant new occupations. People became more independent and no longer had to rely on a lord for land. As international trade rose in the fourteenth century, sawmills played an important role in preparing lumber for shipbuilding. International trade also meant contact with other cultures, which influenced life, art, and architecture in medieval Europe.

The water mill was adapted to produce other types of goods besides flour. Water mills, for example, helped transform the growing textile industry. At textile mills, called fulling mills, freshly woven cloth, soaked in water, was beaten to compress the fabric and to increase its durability. Hammers replaced the grindstone, and hydraulic energy was used to power the striking action.

Engineers found other uses for the hammer device used in the textile mill. Tanning mills produced leather, and paint mills made dye from plants. Eventually, mills for mining and metal production cropped up along waterways. In the mid-1500s, water power pumped the bellows of a furnace to melt metal for cast iron, and hammers could produce wrought iron, scythes, pins, and needles. Mills also manufactured gunpowder and paper, which helped usher in the Industrial Revolution of the eighteenth century.

Each innovation made mills more efficient. Grain mills started using multiple sets of millstones to increase their output. In 1777 the invention of the steam engine made it possible to pump water back through the waterwheel, keeping the mill in operation even when stream flow was insufficient. In the mid-1800s, wooden parts were replaced by cast-iron parts, which lasted longer and were more efficient.

These advances made the independent miller obsolete. Mills got bigger and more efficient. The price of flour fell, and the individual miller could not keep up with large-scale production. By the 1800s, few small grain mills operated at full capacity in Europe.

# Glossary

**abbey:** A place where monks live.

**apprentice:** One who learns a craft by working with a skilled professional.

**artisan:** A person skilled at a certain craft.

**Benedictine:** A monastic order, noted for ceremonial worship and scholarly activities, that was founded by Saint Benedict in the sixth century.

**bran:** On cereal grains, the edible seed coat, which was usually separated during sifting.

**capital:** In construction, the head or crowning feature of a column. The name comes from the Latin word for head.

**cereal:** A grain that grows on a plant (such as a grass) and is ground for food. **Wild cereal** grows naturally. Over time, people learned how to plant crops and could rely on **cultivated cereal** instead of produce that grew wild.

**feudalism:** The land-based governing system that operated in Europe from the ninth to about the fifteenth centuries.

**gossip:** A person who spreads rumors about others. Mills had a bad reputation in the Middle Ages for being places where people got together to chat and to hear the latest news. In one of his sermons, Saint Bernard railed against the idle conversations and the lies that circulated while people were waiting for the flour to be ready.

**grindstone:** One of two millstones that revolves around a stationary stone, cutting and grinding the grain.

**headrace:** A channel of water that is directed into a waterwheel for industrial purposes.

**hopper:** A bin with a funnel that lets the contents pour out. In a mill, the hopper directed the grain to a narrow space between the millstone and the grindstone where the grain was crushed into flour.

**hydraulic energy:** Energy created by the flow of water that powers mills or turns turbines.

**landowner:** Under the feudal system, the owner of agricultural land who had power over every aspect of life on the property and made up Europe's ruling class for 400 years. Feudal landowners, in addition to managing their estates, could tax farmers, demand military service, arrange marriages, and impose judicial decisions.

**lay brother:** A monk who could not read or write Latin. Because of the lack of such skills, a lay brother could not actively participate in religious ceremonies and was assigned chores related to the material needs of the religious community.

**Middle Ages:** A period of European history that lasted from roughly A.D. 500 to A.D. 1500. The height of the period, known as the **High Middle Ages,** was in the eleventh and twelfth centuries.

**peasant:** A person who tills the soil on land that usually belongs to someone else.

**quern:** A primitive hand mill for grinding grain. The user turns the grindstone with a handle to make a course flour.

**quintain:** A padded revolving dummy set on a pole. Medieval knights honed their fighting skills by charging the dummy on horseback with a lance. A knight's failure to hit the target squarely in the chest caused the dummy to spin. One of its arms, holding a lance or a heavy bag, would then strike the knight in the back as he rode by. This was also a popular children's game.

**Renaissance:** A period of European history that followed the Middle Ages and blended into the modern era.

**Roman Catholic Church:** A Christian religious organization that was founded in the late Roman Empire. After the empire's fall in the fifth century A.D., chaos followed. The Catholic Church became the main source of leadership, political power, and education until the feudal system evolved in the ninth century.

**secular:** Not related to a specific religious order.

**semolina:** A granular powder of ground wheat used especially for making pasta.

**servitude:** A condition in which someone who owes money, usually to a feudal overlord, pays off the debt with manual labor.

**spelt:** A grain, similar to wheat but richer in vitamins, that is no longer cultivated. In the milling process, the bran of spelt tended to stick to the grain, which made sifting more difficult.

**St. Peter's Day:** A holiday celebrated on June 29 in honor of Peter, one of Jesus' apostles and the first pope (head of the Roman Catholic Church). A second St. Peter's Day was held on August 1 to celebrate another aspect of the saint's life. Many religious holidays existed in the Middle Ages. Church bells rang to remind people that this was a religious day and that they should refrain from work.

**tenant:** A person who works on land owned by another and who pays rent in the form of cash or a share of what he or she produces. In the Middle Ages, a lord had many tenants doing the work of his estate.

# Pronunciation Guide

| | |
|---|---|
| *Beaugency* | boh-zah$^n$-SEE |
| *Clémence* | klay-MAH$^n$S |
| *Damian* | dahm-YAH$^n$ |
| *Françoise* | frahn-SWAHZ |
| *Herrard* | eh-RAHR |
| *Isaac* | EE-sahk |
| *Job* | JOHB |
| *Loire* | LWAHR |
| *Matthieu* | mah-TYOO |
| *Nanon* | nah-NOH$^n$ |
| *Notre-Dame* | noh-TRUH DAHM |
| *quern* | KWERN |
| *quintain* | KWIN-tehn |
| *St. Gall* | SAHN GAWL |
| *St. Étienne* | SAHN ay-TYEHN |
| *Vézelay* | vay-zuh-LAY |

# FURTHER READING

**Bussolin, Véronique.** *France.* Austin, TX: Raintree Steck-Vaugn, 1995.

**Curtis, Neal.** *How Bread is Made.* Minneapolis: Lerner Publications Company, 1992.

*France in Pictures.* Minneapolis: Lerner Publications Company, Geography Department, 1991.

**Howarth, Sarah.** *Medieval People.* Brookfield, CT: The Millbrook Press, 1992.

**Howarth, Sarah.** *Medieval Places.* Brookfield, CT: The Millbrook Press, 1992.

**Johnson, Sylvia A.** *Wheat.* Minneapolis: Lerner Publications Company, 1990.

**Kalman, Bobbie.** *The Gristmill.* New York: Crabtree Publishing Company, 1990.

**Langley, Andrew.** *Medieval Life.* New York: Alfred A. Knopf, 1996.

**Patent, Dorothy Hinshaw.** *Wheat: The Golden Harvest.* New York: Dodd, Mead, 1987.

**Patterson, Geoffrey.** *All About Bread.* London: Deutsch, 1984.

# INDEX

# About the
# Author and the Illustrator

**Régine Pernoud,** an internationally known expert on life in the Middle Ages, studied at L'Ecole de Chartres and L'Ecole du Louvre before becoming curator successively of the Museum of Reims in Reims, the Museum of the History of France at the National Archives in Paris, and the Joan of Arc Center in Orléans. A resident of Paris, Ms. Pernoud is the author of more than 40 scholarly works translated into many languages.

**Giorgio Bacchin,** a native of Milan, Italy, studied the graphic arts in his hometown. After years of freelance graphic design, Mr. Bacchin has completely devoted himself to book illustration. His works have appeared in educational and trade publications.